THIS BOOK BELONGS TO:

_____

WELCOME TO TENNESSEE

Dedicated to all the explorers.

All rights reserved.
No part of this book may be reproduced in any form or by any means, electronic or mechanical, and no photocopying or recording, unless you have written permission from the author.

ISBN 978-1-958985-59-5

Text copyright © 2025 by Mimi Jones

www.joeysavestheday.com

A Mimi Book

Tennessee is named after the Cherokee town called Tanasi, which was located on the Tennessee River.

Tennessee was the sixteenth (16th) state to join the union. It officially became a part of the United States on June 1, 1796.

Tennesse is located in the Upper Southern region and is bordered by eight (8) states: Kentucky, Virginia, North Carolina, Georgia, Alabama, Mississippi, Arkansas, and Missouri.

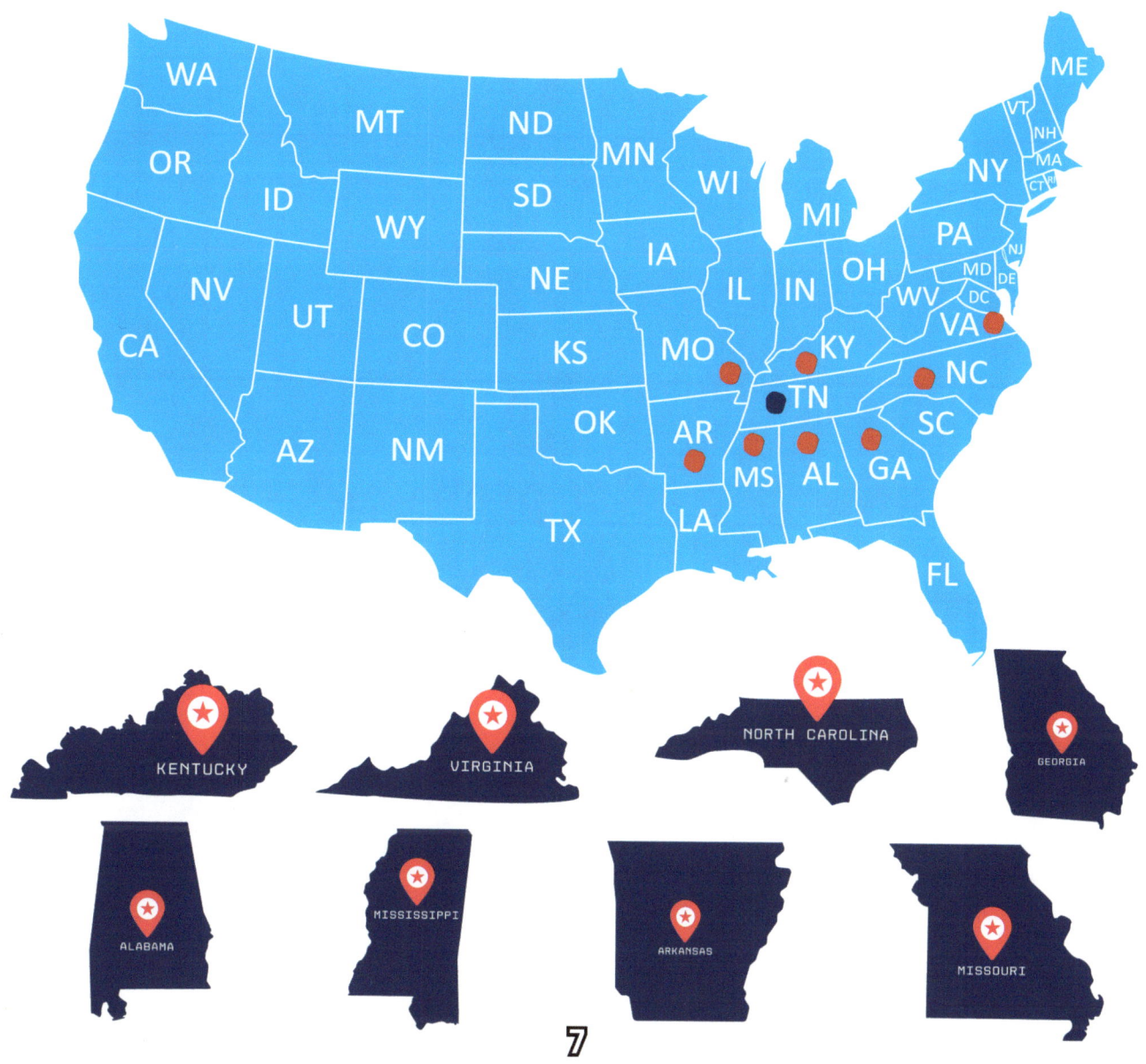

Nashville, Tennessee, has an estimated population of about 1,333,001 people.

Tennessee State Capitol

Tennessee holds the position of the thirty-sixth largest state in the United States in terms of area.

There are about 7,227,749 people who live in the state of Tennessee.

Chattanooga, Tennessee

In 1916, Memphis, Tennessee, became the birthplace of a retail revolution with the opening of the first Piggly Wiggly store. Located at 79 Jefferson Avenue, this grocery store introduced self-service shopping, where customers could pick items directly from the shelves. This simple yet innovative idea forever changed how people shop.

The famous Tennessee Walking Horse is a special breed loved for its smooth gait.

TENNESSEE

Tennessee

There are 95 counties in Tennessee.

Here is a list of 20 of those counties:

Anderson	Greene	Putnam	Trousdale
Blount	Haywood	Roane	Union
Coffee	Jackson	Shelby	Wayne
DeKalb	Loudon	Stewart	Weakley
Giles	Monroe	Sullivan	Wilson

Ruby Falls in Chattanooga is one of the deepest underground waterfalls open to the public.

Tennessee

15

The Great Smoky Mountains National Park has one of the densest black bear populations in the United States.

The Tom Thumb minigolf course, patented by Garnet Carter in 1927, originated on Lookout Mountain in Tennessee and became one of the first standardized minigolf courses to enter commercial mass production.

Elvis Presley, known as the "King of Rock and Roll," moved to Memphis, Tennessee, with his family when he was 13 years old. Memphis played a big role in his music journey; he recorded his first songs at Sun Records there and developed his unique rockabilly style. He later bought Graceland in 1957, which became his famous home and a symbol of his legacy. Elvis lived in Tennessee until his passing in 1977, leaving behind an unmatched influence on music and pop culture.

Tennessee's state bird is the Northern Mockingbird, officially designated in 1987. Known for its ability to mimic over 200 sounds, including other birds and environmental noises, this bird symbolizes joy and freedom.

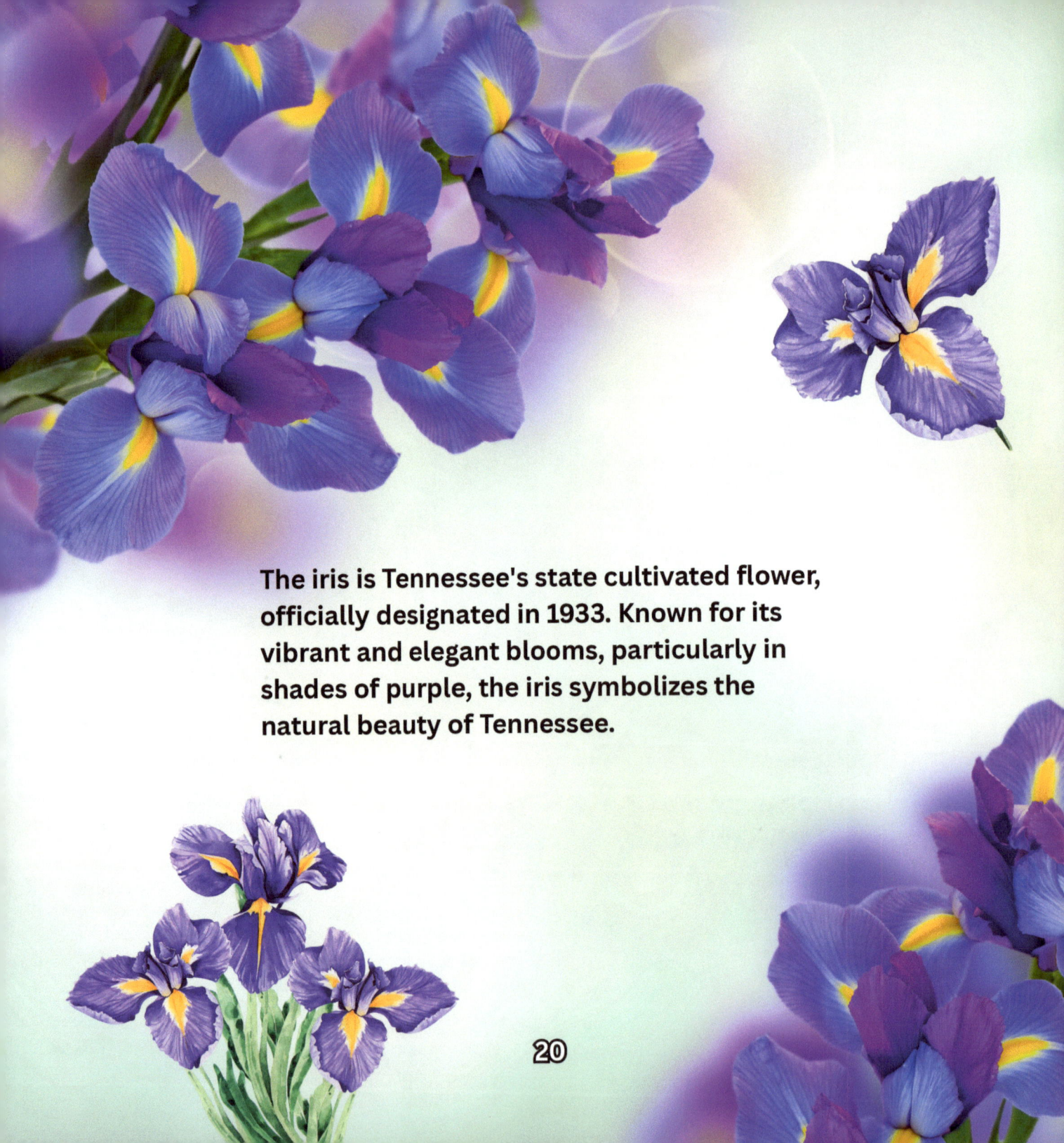

The iris is Tennessee's state cultivated flower, officially designated in 1933. Known for its vibrant and elegant blooms, particularly in shades of purple, the iris symbolizes the natural beauty of Tennessee.

Davy Crockett was born on August 17, 1786, in Greene County, Tennessee, near the Nolichucky River. He grew up in the wilderness and became famous for his hunting, storytelling, and adventurous spirit. He served as a soldier in the Creek War and later as a U.S. congressman from Tennessee. He was known for standing up for the common people. His legendary life ended heroically at the Battle of the Alamo in 1836, where he fought for Texan independence.

Tennessee boasts some interesting nicknames, including the Volunteer State, Little Chicago, and the Big Bend State.

 STATE

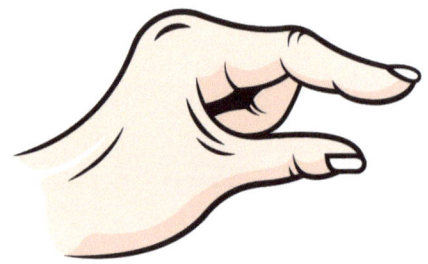 

 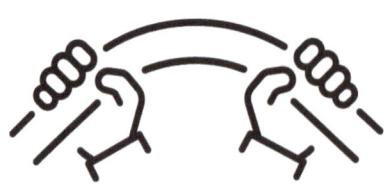 STATE

The Tennessee state motto is "Agriculture and Commerce". This motto, adopted in 1987, reflects the state's rich agricultural and commercial heritage.

TENNESSEE

The abbreviation for Tennessee is TN.

TN

Tennessee's current state flag was officially adopted on April 17, 1905.

Some of the crops grown in Tennessee are apples, corn, cotton, hay, peaches, soybeans, and wheat.

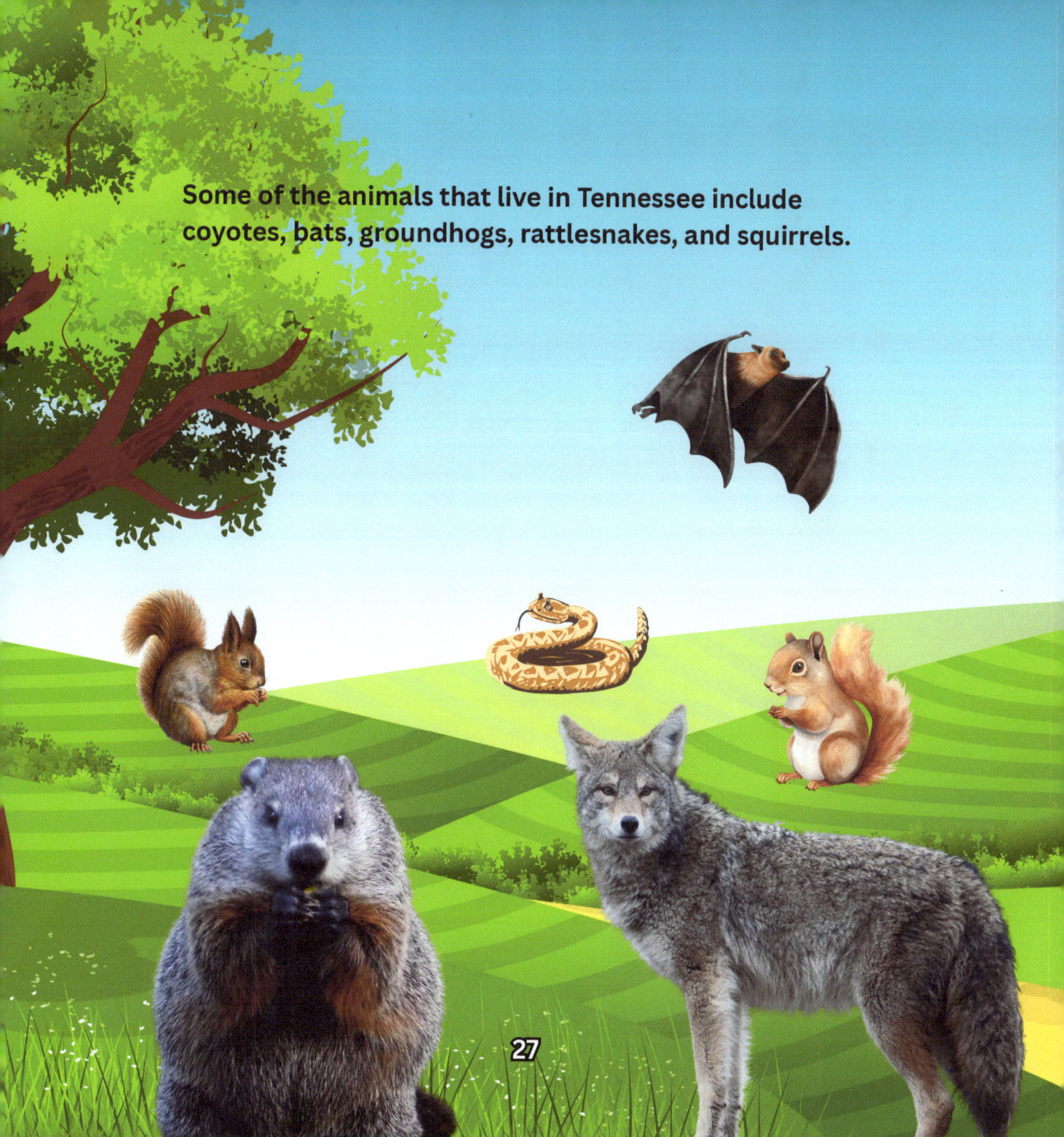
Some of the animals that live in Tennessee include coyotes, bats, groundhogs, rattlesnakes, and squirrels.

Tennessee experiences significant temperature extremes, with a high of 113°F recorded in Perryville on August 9, 1930, and a low of -32°F in Mountain City on December 30, 1917.

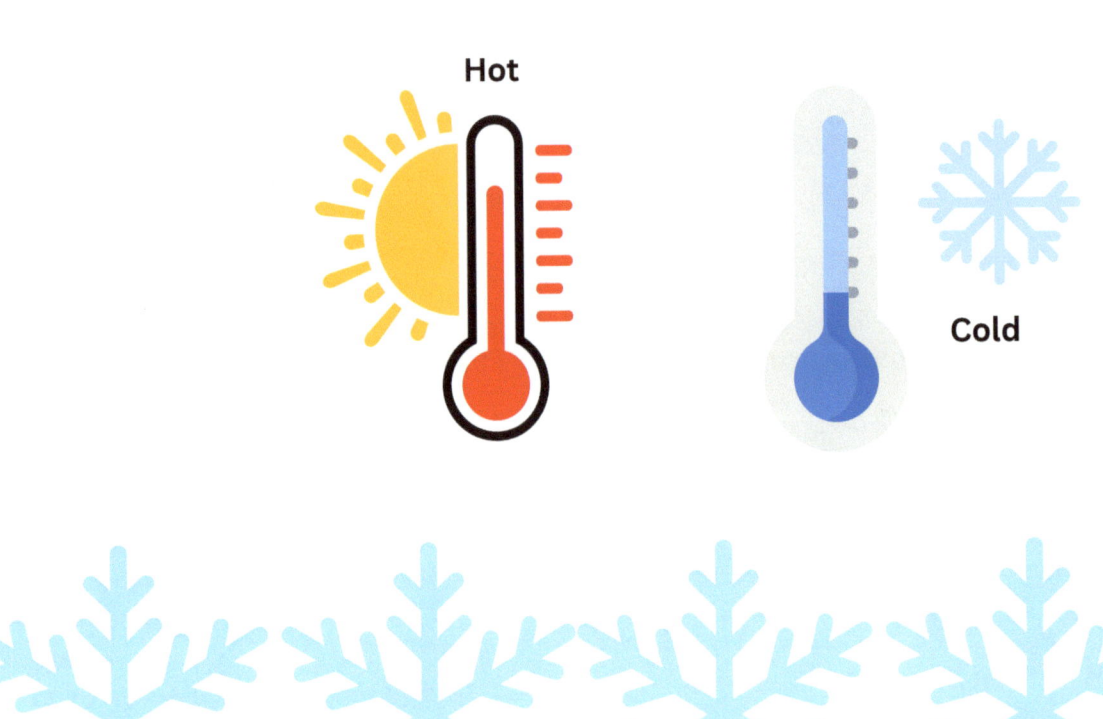

The Tennessee Aquarium, right on the Chattanooga riverfront, is a must-see! It's been around since 1992 and has two main sections: River Journey, which shows off freshwater animals, and Ocean Journey, which focuses on marine life. You can see thousands of creatures there and even catch a show at the IMAX theater. It's all about connecting people with nature and supporting conservation. A true gem in Chattanooga!

Gatlinburg, Tennessee, is home to Ober Gatlinburg, a year-round adventure park with skiing in winter.

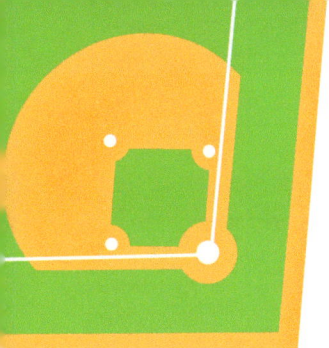

Tennessee has some great baseball teams! There's the Memphis Redbirds, the Triple-A team for the St. Louis Cardinals, and the Nashville Sounds, the Triple-A team for the Milwaukee Brewers. College baseball is big too, especially with the Tennessee Volunteers representing the University of Tennessee.

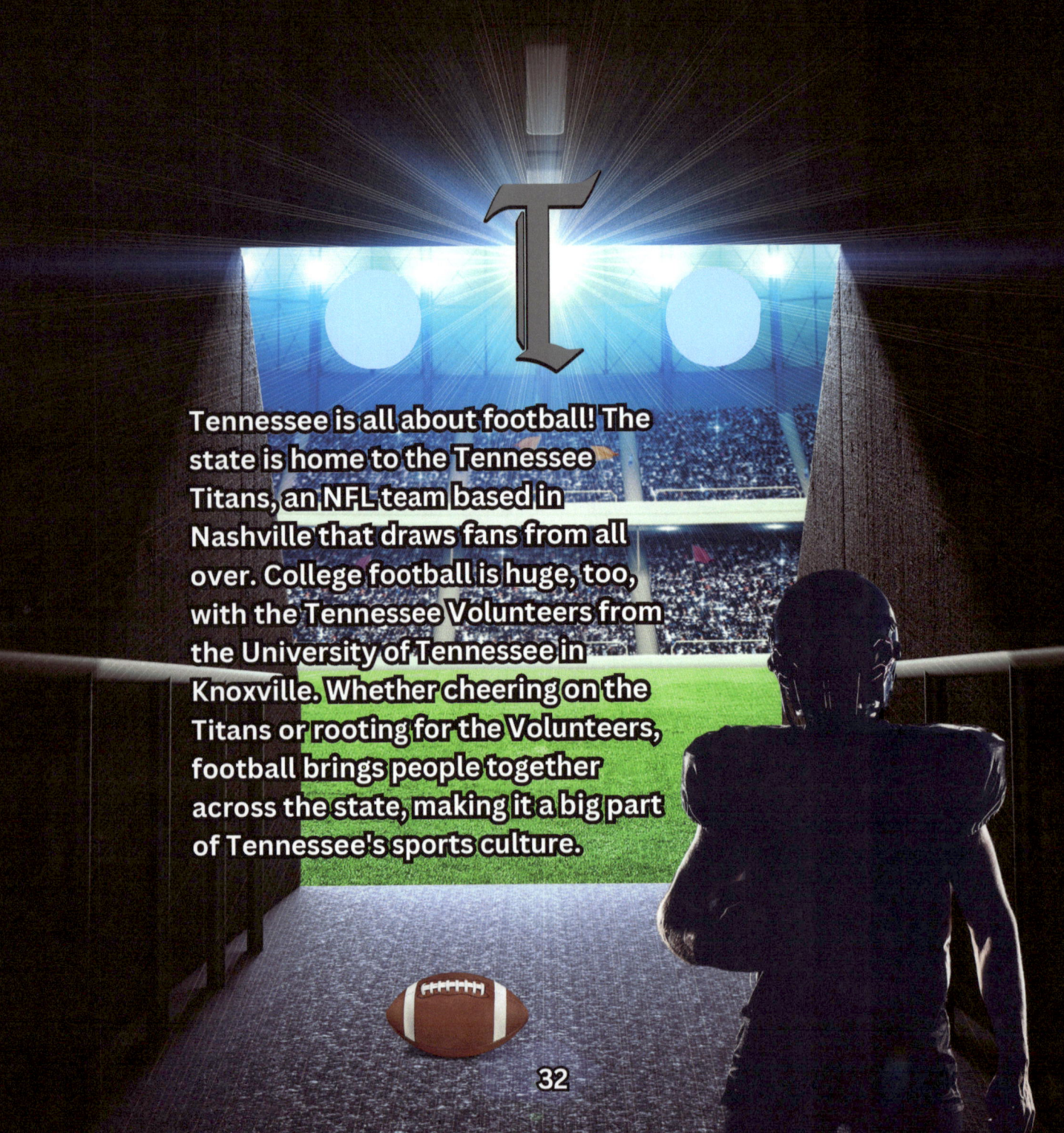

Tennessee is all about football! The state is home to the Tennessee Titans, an NFL team based in Nashville that draws fans from all over. College football is huge, too, with the Tennessee Volunteers from the University of Tennessee in Knoxville. Whether cheering on the Titans or rooting for the Volunteers, football brings people together across the state, making it a big part of Tennessee's sports culture.

Tennessee's Cherokee National Forest covers over 650,000 acres, divided by the Great Smoky Mountains National Park. It features more than 700 miles of trails, seven rivers for whitewater rafting, and over 30 campgrounds, making it an ideal destination for outdoor enthusiasts.

Reelfoot Lake, located in northwestern Tennessee, is a fascinating natural wonder with a dramatic origin. It was formed during the winter of 1811-1812 when a series of powerful earthquakes along the New Madrid fault caused the land to sink. It created a basin that the Mississippi River filled.

Can you name these?

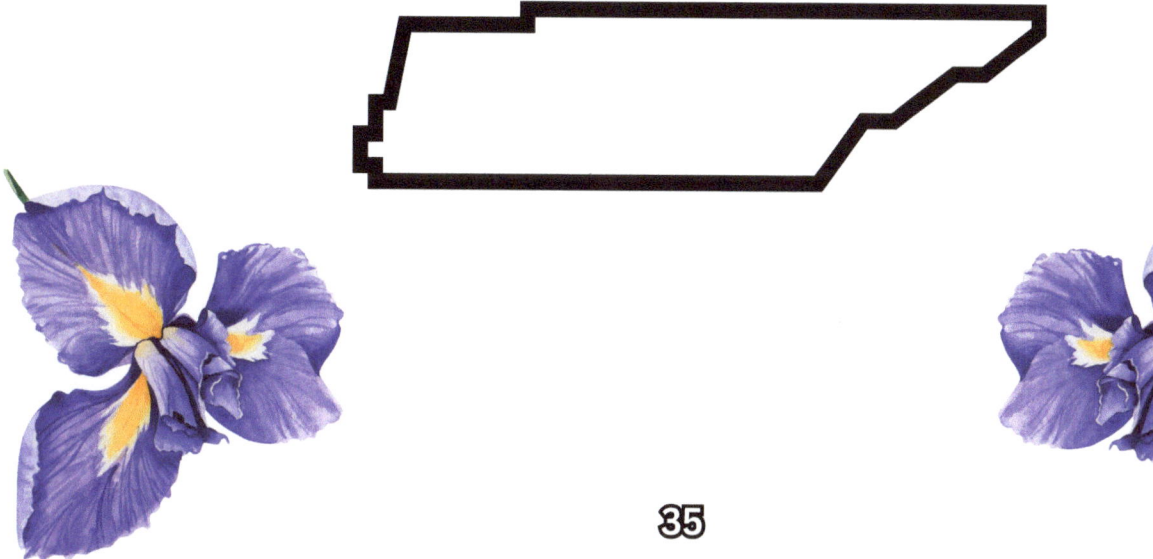

I hope you enjoyed learning about Tennessee.

To explore fun facts about the other 49 states, visit my website at www.joeysavestheday.com. You'll also find a wide variety of homeschool resources to support joyful learning at home. If you enjoyed this book, I would be grateful if you left a review. Your feedback truly helps. Thank you for your support!

Check out these other interesting books in the
50 States Fact Books Series!

www.mimibooks.com